LETTERS TO BOAZ

A heartfelt conversation between Ruth and Boaz

FIRST EDITION Published by Lulu Press, Inc.

3101 Hillsborough St.

Raleigh, NC 27607

www.lulu.com

ISBN: 978-1-329-78146-7

REVISED EDITION September 2019 by Marquia S. Green

Amazon (KDP)

ISBN: 978-1-701-59172-1

Cover design: Ramon Green, *GreenInk*

Cover author photo: Ivy Obasi, *Obasi Photography*

DEDICATION

This book reveals my Journee to my Godly promise.

So many nights have passed by, and I had nothing but the promise of God to hold.

Revelation comes in many forms, but for me I learned to love God with all my heart, mind, and strength. And then, God revealed.

To my promise:

"Suddenly" has captured us; the lovers whose process was long, but manifestation quickly captivated the world before us.

We are far from perfect, but by our thirst for righteousness, we seek God first and trust Him to take care of the rest.

I honor you and together, with God, is "all we need" until the end of time

~Mrs. Green

My Sweet Journee Marie,

Whenever I speak of a journey, I will replace it with your name. I lost you during pregnancy but will remember you forever.

Until we meet again …

I love you,

Mommy

CONTENTS

To Renorda,

I love you so much! Thank you for welcoming me + my family to the church with open arms. My mama always tell me how much she likes "the little me at church." :)

Blessings,
Marquia Green

PREFACE

This book is a compilation of poems, songs, letters, and thoughts shared between me and my husband. It is an opportunity for me to express my deepest love to him and share my love Journee with the world. It is so important to me that he receives the truth in the love within me.

Love for me has not always been easy, as I have faced and conquered many giants. I am neither a worldly licensed psychiatrist nor a clinical therapist, but I am highly learned with experience in heartache and perseverance through God's anointing.

It is only by Christ that I endured the pressures of this world in the name of love. At an early age I suffered loss from what seemed to be everyone I loved.

My first loss was my first love at the age of sixteen. He suffered a seizure in his sleep shortly after he graduated high school. I refused to believe I could live on but I did, and a year later I met the father of my children. We married young and tolerated many sacrifices and compromises just to stay afloat.

We suffered nine years of a tumultuous rollercoaster filled with love, lies, and revenge.

But God was yet faithful.

In 2008 I had enough, and God released me from a difficult marriage.

The only problem was my hardened heart. One night after the divorce, God showed me my ex-husband dying on a table, and when I awoke, I was terrified. Frantically I confronted my ex about the life he was leading. We prayed and we both repented. Two months later it came to pass, and my children's father was gone. I prayed when I first heard the news and begged God to spare his life, but God said, "It is his time." I thought for sure if I accepted my call that God would restore his life, but God did not, and I had to learn to forgive and let God.

A year later, I met someone on the other side of the world.

He was my colleague, fellow service brother, and good friend. We were able to speak life and encouraged one another with the word of God. I could be myself and speak freely of my fears and mistakes in my past. He, too, felt comfortable to lean on me for godly advice, and it was nice.

But I was scared because all I knew was death of the ones I loved, so, I prayed; "Lord, I am afraid to love him because You take everyone I love."

God replied, "The third one I will not take. He will love you like Christ loved the church and will be incapable of hurting you. All you must do is live holy, and I will take care of the children."

From that day forward our love story began, but it was far from perfect. There were many nights of tears and laughter, curses and praise. It would go on this way for seven years until I finally surrendered my last tear.

And through it all I grew stronger.

In a season of grace, God allowed me to know His Spirit deeply. He became my rabbi and I His pupil. And in so doing, I nestled into position to understand the promise that was given to me. I learned how to love God and thus, love was revealed.

My relationship with God has become the strongest it has ever been. Through it all I have learned to accept the gifts God gave me and vowed to endure until the end. God knows it has not been a picnic nor is it one I would have asked for, but I am thankful God saw fit to use me.

I believe my love Journee is a powerful testimony, one that others will greatly benefit from. It is a series of letters to "Boaz," "Ruth," and God that express the realness in true love. I always say real love is not a fairytale. It is more than flowers and candy.

Real love suffers, but it will last for a lifetime.

I am a living testimony. I am triumphant standing on love and promises from God. I pray that every reader will be encouraged by my story and be blessed beyond measure.

Chapter 1: The Hard Year

2008 was a very hard year.

So much was happening I could hardly keep my head above water. But there was purpose.

The kids and I moved to a small town in North Carolina not knowing what was waiting for us. We had much baggage, all full of tears, pain, and underwear. You can never have enough underwear especially if your mom's initials are L.P. But we were there, patching ourselves together waiting for God to send us enough to fill our table.

Why the table you ask? Well, real families eat together at the table. They laugh together, talk about nothing together, and most importantly, they are together! They get to know one another deeply and learn to value what is important to each other. A family that eats together finds *koinonia*—fellowship with the people that matter most. It is offering up your time for someone else's happiness, giving them the best of you.

And when dinner is done, we all can rest knowing that there is a man of God with us who loves us.

I remember walking around the house late at night, wondering what real love felt like—the idea of someone wanting to see what I see, hear what I hear, and most importantly, to feel what I feel. Life for me has not been easy. I have certainly had my share of unpleasant exposure to a great deal of heartache and suffering, and yes, all for the sake of love. I am a lover, one who will empty herself for the hearts and needs of others. What can I say? It is who I am. I believe in it. I hope for it!

And I pray that one day love will find me and rescue me. My Boaz is searching, saving all the love of Christ for me. When I am quiet, I can see him in my mind's eye. He takes his time to know my heart and cares for every one of my needs. He caresses my face just because and whispers "I love you" in his sleep. His favorite touch is while I am cooking, grabbing me from behind to pull me closer for a soft kiss on the base of my neck. And at that moment, I can feel his attraction and it affirms that his love for me is real.

When we are close, he always smells so good and has the most distinguished, imperfect smile that I cherish and make him promise never to correct. His walk is also unique with a sex appeal that intoxicates me.

And he listens. He listens to my heart and takes heed to learn how to love me. It is important to critique what we accept because we teach others how to love us. If we are not careful, we will reap the harvest of the seeds we plant then complain in our own frustration.

But my Boaz is different. He understands and seeks only to fulfill my heart's desires and consults the Word for an example.

Oh, how I love him! I cannot wait to make his acquaintance. When I think of him, my body fills with hope and goodness, and I gasp at the thought of his name. Until I know it, I will call him Boaz and write to him with the prayer that God will bring him my way. I vow now to love him forever and a day if only he knew my name …

But until we meet, he may call me Ruth.

"Beloved, let us love one another: for love is of God; and everyone that loveth is born of God, and knoweth God."

1 John 4:7 (KJV)

19 September 2008

My Dearest Boaz,

As the sun set today, I thought of you. I wondered what you might be thinking ...

Were you preparing your scavenger hunt of love and vows that I long to hear? Do you really see me when you see yourself? Truly I am your reflection.

Can you hear me when I whisper those things that make my heart complete? Do you want me, need me, breathe without me loving you by your side?

I cry out from my loins, "My love, I am standing right here!"

Can you feel me yearning to be first place in your heart beneath only God and His Son? Will you come for me like a prince on a stallion when my soul calls to you at night?

I love you; I want you ... you are my sole desire. Your rib I believe resides in me, and together we are a couple of forever. I so love you, my man, Boaz I'll call you for now. I know in my spirit you are the one God created specifically for me. And I am waiting ... faithfully for you to find me.

Your love,

~Ruth

"And the Lord God caused a deep sleep to fall upon Adam, and he slept: and he took one of his ribs and closed up the flesh instead thereof; And the rib, which the Lord God had taken from man, made he a woman, and brought her unto the man. And Adam said,

'This is now bone of my bones

and flesh of my flesh;

she shall be called 'woman,' because she was taken out of man." Genesis 2:21-23 (KJV)

Living out a suitcase is stressful especially with two high energy kids, but I managed to make it work. We were still pretty new to the area, and I had not pursued opportunities to make any friends. To solve this problem, I invited my childhood friend, who was looking to get away, to come to North Carolina as my nanny. She obliged, and we made base lodging our temporary home.

The kids were pretty good at covering up their grief and extorting me while they did it. A PlayStation 3, Xbox 360, Wii, several Nintendo DS's, two laptops, and three tablets later, I realized I was teaching them to use their hurt to prosper.

I put an immediate stop to it, and my children entered into "Righteous Living 101." I taught them it was time we had a refresher course on why hurt people hurt people. It is not okay to hurt someone just because you have been hurt. We must learn from our suffering and strive to treat others the way we want to be treated, especially the ones who hurt us most.

"Why is it that the people we love most are the ones who tend to hurt us?" I asked. That is a question I often struggle with, but I had to teach my children better. So, I thought, "How will my Boaz treat me?"

God promised me a long time ago that the man He has for me would love me and my children unconditionally and be the head of our house and ministry. God also said the most powerful promise I have ever heard: my husband will be incapable of hurting me. Wow!

What a perfect, imperfect man he must be. Up to this point, hurt was all I had known, but God provided me with the hope of a painless love from a man who lives the Word and will love his wife as Christ loves the church.

1 August 2009

My Darling Ruth,

I see you out there waiting, loving me from so far away.

I wish I could be there to comfort you and assure you all will be okay.

Know that I'm pressing forward, for us, as OUR MASTER demands,

And even though some storms get rough, I'm still moving toward land.

I'm sorry I've been away, especially during those lonely, midnight hours.

But I felt you, I prayed for you as the watchmen covered you from the towers.

I do see you and I hear you, even when you think there's no light.

Know that I'm still coming to find you and to make you my wife.

I love you, you are my choice, in my soul you are my friend.

I will never give up nor settle for less and I'll prove it, but until then ...

I am yours.

Boaz

Inhale ...

It is so hard to feel love from far away. It often feels like a breeze that passes by but does not stay to keep you cool. I remember thinking to myself how life would be if I never found love again. How would my heart beat if he never gave me his rib? I never really thought how life would be if I had it, yet still could not feel his love.

My life has always been hard. Even as a child I struggled with the weights of the world, without even mentioning my own. I always fought tooth and nail for others to prosper but never really fought for my own sake. I imagined that fight to be a battle for my husband, the man whom God says will keep me first after Him.

And there is nothing more attractive than a man of God, my man, standing in the gap on my behalf. To call my name out in prayer and endow me with the rubies and diamonds of a queen's crown. He gets angry when the enemy comes up against me, and when I call him, no matter the hour, he encourages me, prays with me, and most importantly, wars with me against the devil. "Submit yourselves, then, to God. Resist the devil, and he will flee from you" (James 4:7).

He is my protector and seeks only to make me smile. He wants what is best for me and puts me above all others. When he looks at me, I can see that I am truly his desire. I am sexy, intelligent, kind, and sweet, and he loves the way I smile, walk, and speak. He is so in love with me, and it feels good. He regards me as the air he breathes, and I am his Maid Marian in a fairytale made in Heaven.

There is nothing like a man's love, especially when he wraps his arms around me to ensure all will be okay. I so need him! I need Boaz to reset my thinking and spirit to tackle yet another day. Lord knows he can soothe my mind and dissipate my troubles into thin air with just one touch. He makes things better with his presence alone. If only he knew how much I needed that—his presence. To be free to bask in the breath of love, so amazing, so privileged to love like Christ loves.

Exhale ...

Questions to ponder.

Is it possible to place a burden of love on our mate rather than mimic the gift from God?

Why does the Apostle Paul command husbands to love their wives as themselves and wives to honor their husbands?

What does the marriage represent? And how should you reflect it?

"Nevertheless, let everyone of you in particular so love his wife even as himself, and the wife see that she reverences her husband."

Ephesians 5:33 (KJV)

.

Chapter 2: Pause!

"Selah"

Lord, am I wrong for wanting my piece of the pie?

In selflessness that won't occupy too much space of time?

I just want a single bite of my fruition's savor,

to taste it before it loses its flavor.

Is a bite too much if you're called to serve?

Is a morsel much more than I deserve?

Lord, help my hunger! Please help me stay coy!

Help my broken, healed heart unable to enjoy.

A bite is all I desire ... a taste of that which You said was mine.

But if I am in error, cleanse me and help me wait my time.

To accept my promise I cannot touch,

of that which You give requires less of many to give so much.

Selah

"*Charity never faileth: but whether there be prophecies, they shall fail; whether there be tongues, they shall cease; whether there be knowledge, it shall vanish away.*"

1 Corinthians 13:8 (KJV)

Sometimes it is necessary to take a minute to pause, especially when there are so many burdens upon the chest.

I know for certain my chest has loads and loads of unclaimed baggage, and before I realize it, I have burst into a million pieces. It is so hard to put myself together again. Trying to locate and relocate each and every piece of my mind, heart, and spirit is nearly impossible.

Why is that?

Because emptiness cannot mend, only faith and patience, which are usually the first virtues I lose when I am hurting. To be empty is also to be full of nothing and requires me to let go of that which is not and replenish with that which is.

The enemy speaks only in lies, but Christ is the Word of truth. And when Jesus emptied Himself of His divine nature—*kenosis*—He opened the gate for us to be filled with the truth. He gave us passage back to that which is from that which is not.

But it is hard to see truth when I am in pieces and cannot decipher where to put my faith apart from my feelings. I trust God and I am certain God cannot fail, but I am doubtful when it comes to believing for me. With everyone else I rest assured that God is able and willing to do anything but fail, yet I worry when I am in need.

Why God? Why is it so hard to believe for me but easy to believe for the world? How can I be certain for many but unsure for myself?

I so need a fresh anointing.

I need a dose of the breath of God—*ruach*—and a word that only Christ can utter.

A song cries out from my belly:

Hear me Lord, hear my humbled cry.

Hear me Lord, hear my soul in my eyes.

Hear me Lord, hear my voice in all my tears.

Hear me Lord, hear my pain throughout these years.

"*Above all things have fervent charity among yourselves: for charity shall cover the multitude of sins.*"

1 Peter 4:8 (KJV)

"Gray Clouds"

Even when I try to stop crying every, every night,

I can't get out my way … for You to open doors and shine Your light.

But still I give You praise for keeping me even when I couldn't pray.

I appreciate You, even on this cloudy day.

Gray clouds, somehow …

Gray clouds, they seem to always figure me out.

Gray clouds, somehow …

Gray clouds, they seem to always figure me out.

There are times I tried to stop living, giving up, let go of this life.

But I know You're here with me, keeping me through all this strife.

But can I get a break, to love and be loved, one of these days?

On Your time I'll wait … for You, even on this cloudy day.

Gray clouds, somehow …

Gray clouds, they seem to always figure me out.

Gray clouds, somehow …

Gray clouds, they seem to always figure me out.

Gray clouds come but they do not stay, and I pray that God continues to see fit for me to see another day. There is a purpose for the wind and a purpose for the rain. And there is a reason my love for you weathers all storms. I know it may not be easy to understand the raging in my hurricane, but know I am listening, trying and waiting for God to help me answer.

4 January 2011

Dear Boaz,

I've been thinking a lot these days, and my heart has grown weary.

Something happens in the silence that does not always feel so good. "What if I was wrong? What if it were my desires instead of God's?" Those are the questions I find myself continuously asking. It is hard to be faithful when your heart is broken, hard to endure when your eyes and ears do not align with what lies in your heart.

When you see me, will you find favor? Am I to you what the church is to my Savior? So many questions unanswered ... changes, ideas, hopelessness, retreat ... but I am still standing. I am still waiting for you to find me.

I have seen your face, and our daughter's face ... and I have seen the blessings God will unfold. But I saw them as the blind man first saw men, walking around as trees.

God, give me another touch. Spit in my eyes if you must, but help me see clearly!

I still want you, love you. Breathing without you is not an option. There is love here, still, and I'm waiting ...

Forever,

Ruth

"As the Father hath loved me, so have I loved you. Continue ye in my love."

John 15:9 (KJV)

Questions to ponder:

Is it okay to want someone to make you feel better?

Are those called to minister not allowed to struggle with matters of love and relationship?

What does the spirit of heaviness look like to anointed and appointed people? Does it affect their ministry or call to it?

Chapter 3: The Dark Place

Love—why does it hurt so badly?

Why does love feel so good? Why is it so hard to love or be loved when you need it most? I cannot breathe without him, yet I suffocate from his ways. And I am hurting, loving, and praying for brighter days. I cannot decide which hurts more, my pain or his pain—my lack or his lack.

I wish he understood my core and could recognize the depth that it flows. I want so desperately to believe in us because I certainly believe in him, but he just cannot hear me. No matter the volume or melody he still cannot hear the sorrow my flesh feels in only a moment of his wrath. For me it is silence, the wrath of silence that bleeds the ears of my soul.

Lord, help me speak so that he can hear and know that my intentions are pure. Let him see in his mind's eye the love overflowing in me. I come not to destroy or infuriate him, but to give him a lifetime of adoration and honor. I want to bear his child to give the experience every father deserves and afford the opportunity to raise her and train her in the way she should go. I believe there is purpose in her life, because she is the combination of a love's anointing that has not yet been described on Earth.

What we share, even in its anguish, moves mountains and crosses valleys of death. We defy gravity when we are together and bruise the heads of serpents and expose the snares. Why else would I wait, calling you in the beyond, hoping and praying God leads you home? I love you! More than anyone has ever known, a love greater than Hosea, David, and Solomon combined. It is the closest ever to Christ's love for the church, expressed through the heart of a woman.

So, I cannot stray. I cannot leave you. You are me as I am you, so I will dream of you until you find me again and love me the way God intends.

"And now I beseech thee, lady, not as though I wrote you a new commandment unto thee, but that which we had from the beginning, that we love one another."

2 John 1:5 (KJV)

Dear Ruth,

Before I met you, I was in a dark place and had given up on love, thinking it was not for me.

I stopped praying for it and decided I did not want it anymore. I was broken with pieces of my heart spread across the sands of hurt, confusion, and many other things to say the least. I eventually became comfortable in that place and did not mind it. The enemy convinced me that was where I belonged.

But after a while, I started to pray again, and I asked God to show me love. He did. In October, this beautiful young lady came across the world not knowing she came just for me. Neither you nor I understood the purpose God had in mind. My faith was at an all-time low, but you rescued me. All it took was a jump on the back and a kiss on my cheek to know it was love.

We do not always know why God appoints us in a certain place or certain time. We just know we have to fulfill a mission greater than ourselves.

We parted ways not long after, and who would have thought we would cross paths again? But it happened and we talked like we never talked before. At that moment love was stirring. What I thought was the beginning of a good friendship became far more.

But somehow, we lost contact and I remained lost. I just had another child out of lust, and I felt heavily condemned. I had so much anger toward women; so much that I could not explain it, not even to myself. I felt like I was in a box with all my mistakes and very little room to improve.

But then God orchestrated one of us to reach out to the other during a tragedy. You and the children were grieving the loss of their father. It opened up an opportunity for me to console and pray for you and again we talked for hours. It was so beautiful and necessary that it gave me a reason to try again. And when I learned you were close enough to reach, I did so and it felt good.

Love began to stir, but it was not the love I was familiar with. We made plans to see each other and we enjoyed each other's company. Even my reassignment farther away did not stop our love affair. I flew you to visit me, and the time we spent was proof that love was alive again. When you spoke of me with certainty, I knew you were my wife. I have never in a million years wanted anyone like I wanted you. What else could a man want? You sing, cook, clean, are beautiful inside and out. And most importantly you love the Lord.

But as life happened, things started to make us both doubt the love we shared. I made poor choices, and you shut me out. We could not find the utopia we once shared. I want you to know that whatever we go through we must not forget our love. We must learn to speak life into our hearts and relationship so that peace and harmony can reign again. You told me you cannot feel my love and that I hurt you the most. I never meant to hurt you. I love you! I want to make you laugh, smile, and feel all the love I have for you. But If I cannot, I am no longer fulfilling my role as your husband.

You brought me out of that dark place when you agreed to be my wife. Our wedding was the day I saw you in a different light—it was the anointing of God. Although I have seen you operate in God's Spirit before, it was nothing like the way you sang your vows. When I first saw you, I could not contain myself. I saw the glory of the Lord upon you and I was proud to be receiving you as my wife.

Now, I find myself falling back into that dark place. I feel useless and not enough to make you happy. Nothing I say or do is right, and it feels like things are getting worse. But I pray that God restores our marriage so that we remember the love we share. I don't know where this road will lead us, but wherever it goes, please know that I love you.

Sincerely,

Boaz

"Being confident of this very thing, that he which hath begun a good work in you will perform it until the day of Jesus Christ:

Even as it is meet for me to think this of you all, because I have you in my heart; inasmuch as both in my bonds, and in the defense and confirmation of the gospel, ye all are partakers of my grace.

For God is my record, how greatly I long after you all in the bowels of Jesus Christ.

And this I pray, that your love may abound yet more and more in knowledge and in all judgment;

That ye may approve things that are excellent; that ye may be sincere and without offence till the day of Christ. Being filled with the fruits of righteousness, which are by

Jesus Christ, unto the glory and praise of God." *Philippians 1:6-11 (KJV)*

Questions to ponder:

Does love contribute to both joy and pain? If so, how?

Consider the love of Christ as a mirror that reflects His face. Does the love you give reflect the face of Christ?

What should we do when our spouse or loved one can no longer receive the love we give?

"Brethren, I count not myself to have apprehended: but this one thing I do, forgetting those things which are behind, and reaching forth unto those things which are before,

[14]I press toward the mark for the prize of the high calling of God in Christ Jesus.

Philippians 3:13-14 (KJV)

Chapter 4: Pressing Forward

Sometimes before we can move forward, we must return to the furnace and allow God to mold and refine us into the image we were created to be.

Last night I did some soul-searching, and of course right in the middle of my tantrum, God made me minister to someone else. He brought me to the prophet Hosea and his relationship with his wife, Gomer. God told Hosea to marry Gomer even though he knew she was a harlot. Hosea obeyed and loved her but struggled because he knew who she was and the choices she had already made.

I thought about that and asked, "God, why do you make your saints choose a life they know will be hard?" It does not make any sense to me.

I prayed so many nights for God to remove the desire for a child to relieve us from heartache, but nothing happened.

Then God answered, "Because I need to see Me in your words and lifestyle."

With a puzzled face I asked, "What does that have to do with my heart's desire?"

And God said, "Exactly. Do you serve Me because of what I give you? Or do you serve Me because you love Me?"

Wow, talk about pulling my foot out my mouth! I learned quickly that the Holy Spirit surely will cut you if you are not careful. But keep in mind, I was ministering to someone else.

I guess God decided that I needed it more, so He brought to my remembrance the Hebrew prophets in the Word. Every one of them not only spoke the Word from God but lived it. Ezekiel laid in an iron wall for forty days to show the forty years of iniquity Jerusalem would endure (Ezekiel 4:4-5). He was also forbidden to mourn the death of his wife to express God's refusal to mourn over Jerusalem's captivity (Ezekiel 24:16). Jeremiah was also forbidden to marry to illustrate the uselessness of a family when the slaughter of Judah was upon them. (Jeremiah 16:1-13). I was stunned with amazement.

Why would I be any different? Yes, it hurt losing our child, but if I am honest, I was hurting long before we ever conceived.

So, I questioned God again, "Why am I hurting, God?"

And He replied "I allowed it because I am teaching you to cast your cares upon Me."

After thirty-three years, I finally understood the purpose in my suffering. Everything I tolerated was to teach me to trust in the Lord, and if I could endure, so could someone else. My lessons are my testimonies, and my testimonies are my ministry. And through it all, there is hope. God always spoke of hope through His prophets, and God assured me that when the time was right, He would reveal to my husband the promise He made to me.

All I could do was thank Him. So, I said to my Boaz, "I trust God, and I believe that you are he whom God said was mine. You are the one! My husband. And I know so because His word cannot return unto me void and my spirit refuses to let you go."

"*Now will I sing to my well-beloved a song of my beloved touching his vineyard. My well beloved hath a vineyard in a very fruitful hill.*"

Isaiah 5:1 (KJV)

"He Is"

Who's the one my God sent for me?

Who's the one, planted firmly like a tree?

Who's the one, who's upright and tall?

And has answered the Almighty's call?

Who's the one, unafraid to love?

And is worthy of me and all my trust?

Boaz, I know you're out there, and you're looking!

Who is? He is, that's my baby.

Who is? He is, that's my baby …

Who is? He is, that's my baby.

Who is? He is, that's my baby …

He's the one, who will love me.

He's the one, who will adore me.

He's the one, who sees only me

In a room full of beauties.

He's the one, who will share his world.

And he doesn't mind me as his only girl.

God is his moon, and he is my sea,

And I am his waves, a perfect harmony.

Who is? He is, that's my baby.

Who is? He is, that's my baby …

Who is? He is, that's my baby.

Who is? He is, that's my baby …

God knows I love him so. And I am proud that he is my choice and I pray daily, hourly, from moment to moment that what we share will last forever. I am standing on what God promised me!

26 January 2012

My Sweet Ruth,

I know your heart has grown heavy and your patience thin, but please keep fighting our good fight!

I constantly have you on my mind. I can't believe I found someone like you. You are the dream that most men want. I could not ask for a better woman. One day, I hope to become the man of your dreams and be there for you as you have always been for me.

Only God knows what He was doing the first day we met. I knew then that you were my wife! The mere thought of you makes me happy even when happiness could not be found. You make a man's mother love you as if you were her own daughter. With you in the room there's joy to my heart, and I know I haven't always shown it. The touch of your hand brings goose bumps along my spine. You brought back my faith in love I thought I lost. You hold the keys to my heart, and I ask that you drive us straight to Heaven where I'm sure you rest at night. You are that angel on Earth that lovers speak of and I found it—I found you!

Don't ever change. Don't ever allow the enemy to make you feel less than who you are.

You are my Queen, my helpmate, my Ruth. You have humbled my heart and I appreciate you …

I love you always,

Boaz

"Be kindly affectioned one to another with brotherly love; in honour preferring one another."

Romans 12:10 (KJV)

Questions to ponder:

What's the difference between the agape love of God and our emotions?

Can we trust what we feel?

Which is more accurate, the heart or the mind?

Chapter 5: Forgiveness and Reconciliation

Many moons had passed, but a trip to the altar revealed his love was still for me, but in the midst of moving on, he had no peace only shadows and remnants of what was.

There were occasions of reconciliation but never anything substantial. We were reduced to only friends in times of need. I recall a few instances when I needed him and he was there at ten o'clock, eleven o'clock, even midnight sometimes. And he, too, reached out whether in spirit or through my sister, but he always let me know that he needed me and I was there. It was only a matter of time before we both looked back for each other and God made it possible, one day in Charleston. He called me his "Yesterdays" when God spoke to his heart, and with a leap of faith he said:

"My Yesterdays!"

I was thinking the other day about my yesterdays,

How I let my love slip out my life.

They say a man ain't supposed to cry, but ...

When he has lost his love, his heart, and his friend,

He feels like he lost his everything.

So now, he thinks about his yesterdays, and how he's back

Where he has started from: nothing!

No love, no heart, no friend.

It should be easy right?

You've been here, in this same place before.

So, he looks to the Lord in prayer asking,

"Lord, please send me an angel."

As he sits waddled in his tears,

he hears a stilled voice say, "In due time."

He waits patiently only for a moment

just to request for that angel again.

Not realizing rushing a masterpiece can only lead to disaster ...

6 July 2012

My Boaz,

Let me love you.

Let me take care of you and your children.

I am your helpmate.

You'll find favor in me because as I love the Lord, I too will love you. I promise to pick you up when you are down, be strong when you are weak, pray when you cannot, rebuke when your heart is heavy, intercede when the enemy is near, build up when others tear down.

I am your rib as you are the godly head of my house. Let me be your help in times of need. Let me be Eve and you Adam ...

So, let me love you.

Let me take care of you and your children ...

Passionately,

Ruth

"Let him kiss me with the kisses of his mouth — for thy love is better than wine."

Song of Solomon 1:2 (KJV)

Forgiveness is such a blessing to both the giver and receiver, and through forgiveness I finally found my way back to what the enemy tried to steal.

Although I would have never admitted it, during those two years astray, I never stopped loving my Boaz, even when I hardly recognized him. It took much prayer and much faith, but God turned my heart back to him. For so long we lived with two hearts instead of one. We were not designed to live separately, so we were miserable to say the least. This does not suggest that our lives were easy by any means. The shadows from our past haunted us daily along with the frailty of policies in the United States Air Force.

We were finally together again but separated by time and space. And like any other adversary, the enemy took refuge in our division. Loneliness spoke for me, and frustration listened for him. We could not hear love or companionship anymore. We fought like enemies instead of lovers, opponents instead of friends. Life between us was shallow and on the verge of drowning.

"God, please help us remember why we are together! Restore our love and mend our broken hearts." Only God can intervene when we lose sight of the purpose. Only God can renew that which is broken.

So, I remember why I wait so long for my Boaz. Why his smell and smile renew my strength. His touch awakens me from a world of slumber and encourages me to live, write, sing, preach, and be all that God has called me to be. I want to make love to his mind, body, and spirit. I want to captivate every desire and make true every dream and wish he might imagine. I want to feed his belly and his soul and be everything he asks for. I want to be his helpmate, lover, and friend. I want to be his glory as his wife so that every eye that sees me will see God and my husband. He is my only choice and I believe in him, but I need him to receive what I am trying to transmit and not what the enemy wants him to receive.

How do I transmit what I am thinking? How do I communicate so the receiver understands my intent?

When I think of transmitting information, I relate it to my military experience and training. Effective communication is vital for an Airman, Soldier, Marine and Sailor, as we have to be sure our commands are clear and precise. I ponder on the term "transmit" and learn that Webster's defines it as: "to send or convey from one person or place to another (forward)" or "to convey by or as if by inheritance (hand down)."

What does that mean?

As I look deeper and with my military experience, I pose the question; "Have you ever noticed that when people transmit over a hand-held radio, they must press the transmitter when speaking, then release so the message is received on the other end?" That blows my mind!

In other words, to transmit is to send information forward or hand information down. My God! What a revelation for believers! We need both the transmission of the Word (Jesus) that is handed down to us as an inheritance, which we as believers must push forward. And how might we do that? By pressing through until we receive release on the other end. Hallelujah!

This is how I will keep the Word active and moving forward in our lives, relationship, understanding, and ministry. This is how my Boaz will receive on his end. I must press in the Word to allow God to release His promise, our fate, children, and purpose forward. And when it is released, my love will receive.

Thank You, Lord.

30 September 2013

My Dear Ruth,

As I sit here thinking about you, I realized how I was made to love you. You're my destiny.

I can never forget the first time I laid eyes on you. At that time, I did not know we were two ships passing by. It took a year and some life-changing events to bring us together again. I remember calling you my First Lady before you were even my girlfriend. Who would have thought in a million years I would be here, married to the woman I love so dear? It had to be destiny, purpose, God ...

My heart was made just to love you. I receive everything God put in us, and I am thankful for you and His promise.

Forever Yours ...

Boaz

"Seeing ye have purified your souls in obeying the truth through the Spirit unto unfeigned love of the brethren, see that ye love one another with a pure heart fervently." 1 Peter 1:22 (KJV)

[Singing]

Ruth and Boaz, sitting in a tree.

K.I.S.S.I.N.G.

First came love,

and then came marriage...

and hopefully

a baby in a baby carriage.

Lord knows I am so happy to be his wife.

Every day that goes by is blissful because he spiritually and legally belongs to me. We love to be in love. Coming home to him is by far the best part of my day. He is such a baby, but my baby, and I love submitting to my king.

He loves a woman who cooks and takes time to fix his plate, especially when I unwrap and prep his burger for a bite and slip the straw in his drink. He is all smiles from the simple things. I can feel in my spirit when he wants me near and I always know exactly how to comfort him.

When I am in trouble, he calls my name, but when I am in good standing, I am his baby. I know where he has been by the "seat" and the trail of an "Unforgiveable" scent or an oil with the name "Calvin Klein." The sweet ones are my favorite, but he never lets me know which one. It is always a mystery but one I intend to solve.

And he can be a bit frisky, especially when I am frolicking around in my skivvies. I only do it for him, because I love knowing just how much he wants me when I am wanting him. He can never keep his hands to himself, so I expect a pinch on my behind here and there and definitely everywhere …

Yeah, that's my chocolate man. The man of valor God made purposely for me.

Umm hmm, My Man.

It has such a nice ring to it.

[Sings]

I…. I think I found my man.

I…. I really didn't understand …

Ooh, when we first laid eyes,

He was picking my teeth.

And now he's at home waiting for me.

I…. I think I found my man.

I…. I think I love my man.

I…. I think I love my man!

Ooh, he was there when I needed a listening ear.

Scavengers with flowers throughout the years.

I…. I know, I love my man.

I…. I really respect my man.

I…. I really respect my man!

Ooh, he admits when he's wrong and he changed for me.

Now I can be what he needs in matrimony.

I…. I really respect my man!

As with all God's anointed, the enemy wants to steal, kill, and destroy.

It was only a matter of time before life between us went sour. Things that were not an issue before became an issue and it hurt. Soon talking was absent, smiling was scarce, and happiness was MIA. The scripture "Be angry but sin not; let not the sun go down on your wrath" (Ephesians 4:26) was a task. I tried to talk it out, but he could not hear me over his anger. He tried to love it out, but I could not feel it over my sadness.

And the sun set.

"How could this be, Lord, if he is the one?"

We endured everything possible from orders that separated us by 5,000 miles, to therapy, depression, and PTSD. It was bad, really bad, but not in the major things—only the subtleties.

So, I prayed.

One thing I have learned is to listen to the Holy Spirit. When I let go of the hurt, the Lord told me that the enemy is subtle. "Be leery of the subtle things, for over time they become strongholds."

He gave me a vision of a small boy imitating his mother, walking in her heels and playing with makeup. Then later on in his life the child claimed and believed he was "born" a homosexual. All his life he only remembered walking in heels and wearing makeup, so surely it meant he was gay.

But God said, "Not so! I Am just. He only remembers the subtle things. It is in the subtleness where strongholds take root and requires deliverance."

According to Webster's, "subtle" means "to be clever at attaining one's ends by indirect and often deceptive means."

We dismiss the subtle things not knowing how deeply they affect us. And this is true for both the good and bad things in life. Is it not true that we neglect how good electricity is until the lights go out? Or mama's good cooking until we wake up without the smell of bacon?

Apostle Paul states in 2 Corinthians 10:3-4, "Though we walk in the flesh, we do not war according to the flesh, for the weapons of our warfare are not of the flesh, but divinely powerful for the destruction of fortresses [strongholds]."

Paul goes on to describe these strongholds in a metaphor: "We demolish arguments and every pretension that sets itself up against the knowledge of God, and we take captive every thought to make it obedient to Christ" (2 Corinthians 10:5).

These "arguments" are the ideas we in the world develop to cope with life and the situations that arise. The "pretension" is the pride that justifies how and why we choose to cope outside of the Word of God. Subtle moments of anger, confusion, and disappointment easily become strongholds that are designed to separate us, through pride, from God.

We demolish them, Paul so eloquently suggests, by bringing into captivity every thought that rises up against the "knowing" of God who is Christ Jesus. To "know" requires a relationship that needs communication to exist. Communication as dialogue between one another will demolish such strongholds when it is within the Word of God.

Did I read that correctly?

When we discuss our problems before the Lord and find truth within the Word, we eliminate the subtleties meant to separate. So, discuss those subtle things and remove any attempts to grow roots in your life. I will say again, "Be angry, but sin not. Do not let the sun go down on your wrath" (Ephesians 4:26).

So, Boaz, let us settle what is subtle to demolish what separates. We are not defeated. Our love has not gone out but is burning within us, waiting to ignite again.

Questions to ponder:

If marriage ought to reflect the Passion of Christ, what happens when it doesn't?

Is the ministry of deliverance beneficial for marriages that are in trouble?

Can a broken marriage hinder one's purpose and anointing?

My Boaz,

I am grateful to have met you, oh so long ago.

The blessings and the trying times have definitely made us grow.

I am thankful for the Journee, and I am blessed with you as my friend.

My heart and soul have chosen you, from now until the end.

I am humbled by your faith and prayers, and all the love you've given.

And I know it hasn't been easy, loving me and my bad decisions.

Of course, we are not perfect, we must both share the blame.

But I am in love with my "Boaz," whose name is really Jermaine.

No matter the valleys' depth, or the height of the mountain tops,

God is not yet through with us; our purpose cannot be stopped.

Our love must be eternal, because nothing can taint its shine.

The moment we said "I do," we should last forever and a lifetime.

I love you,

Ruth

"Husbands, love your wives, even as Christ also loved the church, and gave himself for it;

That he might sanctify and cleanse it with the washing of water by the word,

That he might present it to himself a glorious church, not having spot, or wrinkle, or any such thing; but that it should be holy and without blemish.

So, ought men to love their wives as their own bodies. He that loveth his wife loveth himself.

Ephesians 5:25-28 (KJV)

<u>Chapter 6: Revelation</u>

But then there was smoke. The flame had gone out and there was nothing left to ignite it. Time had created so much silence between us that we no longer recognized each other's voices. Heartbreak is the only sound I hear along with anger and regret. Carnival cruises were one-sided, and voicemails boxes were full of disrespect and tears. The hope for a baby was recanted and I felt betrayed. Love didn't live here anymore.

My children became receptors to many broken pieces. By day I worked into the night and by night I cried into the day. It wasn't healthy. I knew I had to lay before the Lord as He was the only refuge available to me. For weeks, I fasted by default and cried out from my belly, "Father, where are you? Take away this pain. I don't want my promise anymore."

At first, there was no response, just more unbearable silence. But then God began to deal with me concerning who I was pretending to be. PRETENDING! The nerve; after all the pain I endured on the account of a promise: *"The third one I will not take. He will love you like Christ loved the church and will be incapable of hurting you. All you must do is live holy, and I will take care of the children."* It just didn't make any sense. I was furious. But God spoke again to my spirit: "Why are you looking for Boaz when he was promised to Ruth? I knew at that moment; Boaz wasn't my promise. God would never promise me another woman's husband.

I was committing spiritual covetousness and I needed to repent. The interesting part is that our marriage didn't end there. I continued to fight for the emotions that had me bound. And he toiled back and forth between what he felt and what he thought. His mind was bigger than his heart most days so I could no longer feel any love. All the signs were there. He made it very clear that he did not need me in his life. He stopped coming home, wearing his ring, and communicating all together, but I refused to take the hint. I was so sure he was the one; it made sense for him to love me. And once upon a time I was certain he was my husband. I begged him to come home for the holidays, and on New Year's Eve, the Holy Spirit settled my spirit and I knew it was over.

We spent Christmas in Roanoke, and it was weird but nice. I realized he had barely been home with me our entire relationship. I mostly visited his family, sometimes without him. My family embraced him and his son, who might I add was conceived a few months after we lost Journee, but I loved him so that didn't matter. My only concern was his lack of love for the child we lost. I never showed it to his son, but it was definitely an issue in my heart.

We played games, laughed, and had plenty to eat. It was a great visit home as a family. But we decided to spend New Year's with his family to continue the tradition of watch night at his home church. Earlier on New Year's Eve, I had an uneasy feeling in my stomach. It was a sense of expectation yet fear that stirred in my spirit. My children declined the trip and stayed with my mother so only his son accompanied us. The watch night service was powerful, the Spirit was high, and the love in the air was comforting. But something was still stirring in my spirit. At five minutes till midnight, the lights went out and the church kneeled to pray as the deacons watched the hour approach.

"Watchmen, watchmen, ole watchmen, please tell me the hour of the night. Time moving on, time moving on; five minutes before midnight."

The Holy Spirit began to speak to my spirit, "This is end of this heartache; you will not be here next year."

"Watchmen, watchmen, ole watchmen, please tell me the hour of the night. Time moving on, time moving on; four minutes before midnight."

"I have heard your cry and although I granted his petition, he did not fulfill his vow."

"Watchmen, watchmen, ole watchmen, please tell me the hour of the night. Time moving on, time moving on; three minutes before midnight."

"I release you and it is well. What I promised you is for you. My word will not return unto you void."

"Watchmen, watchmen, ole watchmen, please tell me the hour of the night. Time moving on, time moving on; two minutes before midnight."

"I will heal your heart; for I have come for the brokenhearted."

"Watchmen, watchmen, ole watchmen, please tell me the hour of the night, Time moving on, time moving on; one minute before midnight."

"Peace be unto you. It is well."

"Happy New Year!"

6 February 2016

Dear God,

It hurts so badly. My heart is in pieces and my words have gone astray.

I feel I will die from this heartache, but I know I will not. Yet still I pray that it will go away. It hurts being me, Lord. Why can't You just let me come home? The world thinks I'm strong, but the truth is I am not. This turmoil in my marriage is destroying me. My husband cannot hear me and chooses not to know my name. He has given me away in his heart a long time ago and now I am last. Today, I felt it when he walked in and out again. There is no love here, only pride. Lord, I have no more words. My faith and hope are saturated with anguish. All I have is one last cry and with it I have no words. All I have is what Your Spirit will offer ... JESUS, please help me!

My spirit cried out, and the Holy Spirit spoke on my behalf. A heavenly language filled my belly and poured off my tongue. For twenty minutes my spirit emptied unto the Lord, and when it was over, I was done. Two months later we were divorced, and I was at peace.

I decided to continue to seek God and minister wherever the Spirit led me. I was no longer looking for Boaz or anyone for that matter. I was busy spending time with me, and that's when I met him. He was where I used to be. I noticed his social media post full of poetic sorrow and yearning to get closer to God. He was my military fraternity brother and I was his sister. I felt good about encouraging him as he did me. I never thought a few months later he would be the answer to my prayers.

God reminded me of my promise, *"The third one, I will not take. He will love you like Christ loved the church and will be incapable of hurting you.*

All you must do is live holy, and I will take care of the children."

Immediately the enemy stepped in and tempted us. A part of me was so happy to be sinful just to feel the embracing arms of a loving man. But I knew it was wrong and although my conviction didn't kick in right away, it wouldn't take too long to catch up to me. We reevaluated our relationship and began to put God back in His rightful place.

He was a breath of fresh air and I needed to breathe. He wasn't looking for a girlfriend nor was I looking for a man; we both were looking for a Word from God. He was in his secret place on the floor, hearing from the Lord. And I was in my secret place praying to the Lord. I was in a season of worship and study, and he was in a season of humility and submission. Both searching. And we found a reason to love, again.

"For this reason, shall a man leave his father and mother, and shall be joined unto his wife, and they two shall be one flesh.

This is a great mystery: but I speak concerning Christ and the church.

Ephesians 5:31-32 (KJV)

"Reason to Love"

Is there ever a reason too good to love?

That makes burdens of broken pieces, fall together above,

That which doesn't stick to or even keep to, what one thought just because,

Trusting in a dream of forever that ended quickly before it ever was.

Two doves, no turtle, just two winds without flight.

In a heaven without twinkling stars to shine bright throughout the night.

Just hopeless aspirations of a maybe or a might, with a strong possibility of a future of ridicule and strife.

A new ending is needed with a beginning that weathers the storms; of separation, degradation, manipulation, and reform.

A kiss on the forehead and sweet calls in the late night; from a lover who is faithful, always grateful, lovingly mate-ful, even when it isn't right.

So, is there a reason too good to love?

Only if the reason is in the season, I can believe in, came from above.

R.E.S.P.E.C.T. came in to save me, laughter pushed through and made me whole enough that maybe God will give me another baby, to hold in my arms beside the man who transformed me,

Into the reason, in this season, I can believe in, to be love.

He and I are the latest outfit, and most of our friends and family are excited. Most importantly, we are Bible study buddies and my newest best friend (BFF, don't worry you're still my BFF).

We literally talk about everything. Again, my heart begins to fall but I am leery, and I do not trust it. Despite my hesitation, he tells me, "You are all I need." When I ask how he can be so sure, he says "Because you confirmed what the Holy Spirit told me." During one of his many dates with God in his secret place, he posed a series of questions to the Lord:

1. Is he forgiven of his indiscretions from his previous marriage?
2. Is it not good for a man to be alone?
3. Would God bring him a woman of God?

By the Spirit, God answered yes to all his questions. So, he vowed:

"The woman of God I am given, I will love her like Christ loved the church. But how will I know when I find her?"

God answered, "She will be all you need."

One day he and I were texting, and I was smitten by our conversation. I decided to spice things up a bit, so I went into character of all the hats I carry. I wanted him to know that every part of who I am as a person appreciated who he was as a person. Words are our strong suit since we are poets in nature.

I introduced myself as Evangelist Marquia, the minister who will cover him with the word and prayer. Dr. Marquia, the educated woman of stature that will reflect him well amongst the masses and give honor to his name. Soror Marquia, who as his sister will be his keeper and have his back. Mrs. Marquia, the wife and good thing that brings favor of the Lord. All in all, "Baby, I am all you need."

At that moment, his spirit quickened to the Word given by the Holy Spirit and he knew I was the one. From that day forward, he prayed for me and our union to be blessed by the finger of God. Daily he covered me, and I didn't even know it until the Spirit and my nosiness led to his prayer journals. He prayed for my peace, healing of my heart, clarity of my mind, focus of my ministry, and direction of my feet! Glory to God! He literally fulfilled every portion of God's promise to me to include a baby girl.

He and I have something that God ordained and it's beautiful. It isn't always peachy, and there are some days I want Calgon to take me away. But at the end of the day I know there is a man of valor sleeping next to me. There is a man of God praying for me and our children. There is substance to him that rests in the promise of the Word. And I can say with certainty that he fulfills God's promise to me but most importantly, I have finally reached the right position to receive my gift from God.

This process was not to seek a man, but to seek out the face of God to trust Him that He will do just what He says He will do. I learned a lot about me on this Journee. I discovered how to love God with my whole heart, mind, and strength. I increased my faith to a level beyond my emotions and revealed the secrets to waiting on the Lord. I discovered the joy of the Lord and endurance of pain to plow the way for my mantle. My promise was a confidence course in Jesus that built a virtuous woman, a wife who is finally ready to receive her blessing.

Of course, this does not mean that things are easy. Life is not perfect nor is it without struggles and hard work. But I am clear on the woman that I am, and I have opened my heart and spirit to receive my God-given promise. I am changed. Finally, I have become a wife ready to receive her husband.

Questions to ponder:

Can you receive blessings while committing sin?

Should healing occur before a new relationship or because of a new relationship?

Is peace an indicator of God's will? And can it be imitated by the enemy?

<u>Chapter 7: My Answers to the Pondering Questions</u>

<u>Chapter 1 Questions to ponder:</u>

Is it possible to place a burden of love on our mate rather than mimic the gift from God?

Absolutely! Love is tangible and by far the greatest gift of the Holy Spirit as stated by the Apostle Paul. But love is a choice. It is solely up to the giver and not the responsibility of the receiver. As believers, we are called to love our neighbors and enemies and the Word says to do so "as thyself." In other words, the burden of love should never be placed upon anyone but ourselves. But we all do it, because we desire to receive what we give. I believe God has called us to choose to love our neighbors because it is the likeness of who He is, and we are created in His image. Marriage and relationships should start with the choice to love like Christ to be pleasing to the Father and in doing so, we will love one another without placing any burdens on the other. Love is a gift and a privilege to have.

Why does the Apostle Paul command husbands to love their wives as themselves and wives to honor their husbands?

The Church of Ephesus is the epitome of love. Beginning with the Apostle Paul, then Timothy, and later Apostle John—all beacons of the same love motif. I don't find it a coincidence that Apostle Paul would address love in his epistle. Ephesus was a thriving city full of Greco-Roman influence, and temptations of the church's "old selves" were just outside the front door. I believe Apostle Paul's address to the family was intentional because marriage is the reflection of the Passion of Christ which is to the church. He calls husbands to love their wives as Christ loved the church and as they love themselves. He is addressing the original mandate placed upon man given to Adam in the Garden of Eden. He is referencing the image that man was created in and the position he was given to "cultivate woman and become one flesh." We forget that Adam was the first gardener and given dominion over everything on Earth. God charged man to cultivate, to promote growth, and it is his responsibility to care for the seed until it becomes the tree. The same is true for a husband and his wife. He is responsible to nurture her to be the best she can be so that she may be presented "without spot or wrinkle." The Passion of Christ illustrates the love of Christ for His bride—the church. And it agrees with the mandate given to Adam in the beginning.

A wife, the Apostle Paul says, should honor her husband because he cares for her, maturing her into the flower God has destined her to be. Honor is what builds and manages the will to remain humble so that the Spirit can migrate through. The wife is also called to be the husband's helpmate, which is often taught incorrectly as synonymous. Untrue. Husbands are not the helpmate to the wife, but the wife is the helpmate to the husband. God has done so because favor is embodied in the bosom of the wife. Why? Because she will bear the seed that will strike the serpent's head. Woman carries the womb that brought forth the Savior to the world and therefore has the favor of the Lord. To carry that much grace requires honor, and it should be rendered first unto God and then to her husband. Men respond to honor like women respond to love. He requires it in order to stand as the head of the household. To be the recipient of instruction for the family, a husband needs the honor of his wife to be the man of valor God created him to be. She is what is missing, because she came from his side.

The Apostle Paul understood that the church of Ephesus had a love problem. Jesus would prophecy to the Apostle John on the island of Patmos about love in Revelations 2:4-5: "...Nevertheless I have somewhat against thee, because thou hast left thy first love. Remember therefore from whence thou art fallen, and repent, and do the first works; or else I will come unto thee quickly, and will remove thy candlestick out of his place, except thou repent." Jesus warns the church of Ephesus to remember their first love, who is Christ, lest their favor will be removed.

It is important to understand the roles of the husband and wife because they ultimately reflect the Passion of the Christ.

What does the marriage represent? And how should you reflect it?

Yes, you guessed it! Marriage represents the Passion of the Christ and should reflect the love Christ had for the church, who is His bride. Everything rendered within marriage should be done first unto God and in doing so, both husband and wife will fulfill their purpose to each other and to God.

Chapter 2 Questions to ponder:

Is it okay to want someone to make you feel better?

Of course! Humans are relational because we were created in the image of the Triune God. In the Godhead, there is oneness and unity that equates to one being that is God and three distinct persons that are the Father, Son, and Holy Spirit. There is a relationship within the Trinity that operates in love and that is exactly why we must do the same. Christ calls us to kindness which is part of the biblical definition of love. Whether it is philos (friendship), eros (romance), storge (affection), or agape (unconditional), love requires relationship. It is human to want kindness, and it is a requirement to love others. What we do unto others, we also do unto Christ. He [Jesus] said that, not me. Jesus said, "Give to the least of these ..." in Matthew.

In marriage, the other spouse should always be the most important person in your life. How they feel reflects many things, and it is imperative that the other spouse is attentive to their mate's concerns.

Are those called to minister not allowed to struggle with matters of love and relationship?

I remember going through some really hard days during my failed relationship, and it was difficult to separate my emotions from my sleeves. One of my closest friends and Ladies Tea Time members also struggled with my difficulty to do so. One day at work, my broken heart was written all over my face, and my friend immediately rebuked me. Flowing from a mixture of disappointment and compassion, she exclaimed; "How are you in this place? I thought you were saved ... I thought you were a Christian." My first response in frustration was, "I can't have a bad day because I'm saved?" How unfair and unfortunate if that were true. But what I realized is that I was an ambassador of hope to all those who were searching to believe. Although it was a misplaced and incomplete understanding of the Christian faith, it was flattering to say the least. What I learned from it was that who we are in Christ is greater than what we are for ourselves if they are out of alignment with God's will for our lives. So, what does this have to do with the aforementioned question? Matters of love and relationship should be the residual of seeking the kingdom of God and His righteousness as expressed in Matthew 6:33. To say that neither party will succumb to his or her fleshly selves and fall short at some time is unrealistic because at the end of the day, we are all in fact, human. Humanity, who have been redeemed, has a responsibility to resist its sinful nature to draw nearer to the design of the Creator. Struggling to love one another is not a problem with one another, but rather an issue in priority. When we seek God first, we will find love, affection, comradery, and peace in all our relationships because our priorities will be in their highest and most effective order possible.

What does the spirit of heaviness look like to anointed and appointed people? Does it affect their ministry or call to it?

The spirit of heaviness is first and foremost not of God. Like all evil spirits, the spirit of heaviness is a person without a body that desires to burden a person with unnecessary loads of distraction and delay with the ultimate goal of destruction. Every assignment of the enemy is to kill, steal, and destroy, especially the anointed and appointed in Christ. Heaviness is designed to deter them from fulfilling their purpose in Christ and lead to a premature death. But Christ refuted this very spirit the day He taught from Isaiah 61 in the synagogue. I find it appropriate that this passage in Isaiah describes how to triumph over the spirit of heaviness, and Jesus declared in Luke 4:18-21 that He has fulfilled it. In other words, Jesus asserted that the scripture that speaks of the hope and comfort of the Lord to those that mourn has been fulfilled. The hope is the garment of praise. Everyone, especially the anointed, must put on the garment of praise to overcome the weights of heaviness. It can absolutely affect their ministry and calls to it in the sense that the enemy is attracted to the anointed because he has limited time on Earth. The spirit of heaviness is an accomplice of the python—divination whose purpose is to choke out the breath or anointing. Its goal is to distract so it can choke out the anointing and ultimately kill the spirit. Fortunately, it does not have the authority to kill our spirit because our spirit is in the holy of holies. But we have the power to do so in our free will. That is why it is important to keep on the garment of praise to fine-tune our hearing so that we can discern the voice of the Lord from all others.

Chapter 3 Questions to ponder:

Does love contribute to both joy and pain? If so, how?

The Bible describes joy as it pertains to God and says, "it is our strength" (Nehemiah 8:10). The Bible also touches on pain in this same passage during a season of pain for the Israelites. Nehemiah records the public reading of the Law in this passage as Ezra, the priest and scribe, blessed the Word of God and read the Law to the exiled people. They were reaping from their disobedience and felt a loss of identity and covenant as exiles. But hearing God's word brought an understanding that was filled with hope and restoration in the midst of their warranted circumstance. *Their understanding provoked weeping and repentance which therefore can be forgiven. And in forgiveness, there is restoration.*

We know the end of the story that leads to Jesus' crucifixion and resurrection, which epitomizes this restoration and causes a buildup of joy or gladness in expectation. Jesus is the Word in flesh and He is also the love that fulfills and causes the expectation of God's restoration in our lives. So yes, love contributes to joy and pain because it can be present in them both. It takes understanding to move from pain to joy, but love is still present. Just as the people had to gain understanding in their error to see the pain they caused the Father, it shifted to joy once they understood that God still loved them despite their actions. The same is true in relationships. I could not feel any love, only pain and he could not give me more than I could understand. What we had was not a love issue, but a misunderstanding and unfortunately it cost us our marriage.

I sought him to love me and he sought me to understand him, but neither of us sought God to find the joy that was our strength. Strength is what we needed to love and understand one another to weather the storms that were coming to face our marriage.

Consider the love of Christ as a mirror that reflects His face. Does the love you give reflect the face of Christ?

The love of Christ should reflect His face as He walked on this earth, especially in a marriage. How we choose to love others serves as a mirror to the God or gods we serve. If what we give only benefits us, then who we serve is selfish. But if what we give is beneficial to others, then who we serve is selfless. Jesus came as the Son of God yet washed the feet of men. He healed the blind, deaf, outcast, and demonized, and walked with the poor, common, and unlawful. He was a king with a servant's heart, and that is what makes all the difference.

When we love only to gain, we lose the face of Christ who was obedient to what He saw His Father in heaven do. In marriage, love your spouses because God the Father loves them and serve their hearts the way they can understand. The Bible teaches specifics on the roles of the husband and wife, and if we honor that, God will honor us in our efforts to give love that reflects Christ's face.

What should we do when our spouse or loved one can no longer receive the love we give?

If we have adhered to the biblical mandate in our position and have released our spouse or loved one to God on the altar, then the rest is up to God. I am not an advocate for divorce, but I am one for peace. I believe God will make clear and order every man's steps who are righteous. If we are led by the Spirit of God, we will not be led astray. This does not always mean it's time to leave, but it surely means it's time to listen. The soul is full of emotions and thoughts that are not always fixated on Jesus, so it is best that we lean not to our own understanding but seek God for clarity. In the meantime, we ought to practice what God has mandated in us and be the best wife or husband we can be until God makes it plain.

Chapter 4 Questions to ponder:

What is the difference between the agape love of God and our emotions?

The main difference between the agape love of God and our emotions is that one is unconditional and the other is conditional. But more importantly, agape love is restricted from the emotions. It is a selfless love that gives willingly despite the response or lack thereof within the emotions or soul. Agape comes from the spirit that is willing to love regardless of the circumstances. I believe agape love is permanent because it either is or is not. It is not something that can turn on or off but is a choice that is accepted or rejected. Once you have it, you have it because it is eternal.

Most people say they want agape love, but what they really desire is eros love or philos love. They want the love that feels good most but expect it to serve eternally or unconditionally like agape—but it doesn't. Agape love does not rest in the emotions like the other types of love: eros, philos, and storge. *They are experienced by how they make one feel while agape love is not experienced but operates in the knowing of what is true. You can count on agape love because it tangibly exists in your being. You know that it exists whereas the other three must be felt or experienced to be realized.*

Jesus knew He had to die for our sins, and He accepted that even in His agony. He made the choice to love us more than what He felt in His carnality. And He gave tangibly everything He was for the benefit of all humanity.

Can we trust what we feel?

I did not understand this when I decided to marry my ex-husband. He felt like my promise, and I wanted more than anything to have what was mine. I did not know in my Spirit because I could not get past my emotions. So, when the smoke cleared and the newness faded, I knew nothing and therefore I had nothing. I did not try the spirit by the Spirit to see if it was good. That is why we ought to guard our hearts and all our gates to our spirit so that we can discern what thus says the Lord from what thus says ourselves.

Emotions are temporary and therefore should not be a resource of revelation. We must stand on what we know is true, and that is what lies in the spirit sealed by the blood of the Lamb. Our hearts are deceiving because it responds too often to what we feel and not what we know, when we are not led by our spirit-man. The Apostle Paul urges us to etch the Law [Word] on our hearts as we are now under the grace of the New Covenant in Christ Jesus. This allows the heart to surrender to the Christ and be enslaved to the will of God. Scripture says in the Gospels, "For out the abundance of the heart, the mouth speaks" (Matthew 12:34; Luke 6:45). If we surrender our hearts to the love of Christ, the mandate of the Word of God's law will come forth.

Which is accurate, the heart or the mind?

I have learned that accuracy is not always truth. Sometimes, what is accurate may not actually be what is truth especially when it comes to love. We are imperfect, so mistakes will happen, but that does not always mean that the truth is that we do not love. This question is pretty loaded to say the least, but it's a great start to a deeper understanding. Both the heart and mind can be misleading because the heart is deceptive and the mind needs renewing. They both must surrender unto the Lamb of God. When we are saved, our spirit is sealed with the blood of Jesus, but the mind and body must follow suit. It is a process that continues from glory to glory or until we "scarcely make it to heaven."

Chapter 5 Questions to ponder:

If marriage ought to reflect the Passion of Christ, what happens when it does not?

Marriage was designed to reflect the union of family and oneness that was created in the beginning with Adam and Eve prior to the Fall. Jesus reestablishes this union of oneness as He suffers for the sake of the church—His bride. Jesus covers the church with His blood to present her without spot or wrinkle, but it was not an easy task. This notion ought to be replicated in the marriage between man and woman becoming husband and wife—one flesh. But this also is not an easy task. Sometimes, the marriage does not reflect the Passion of Christ but rather displays a different message that does not always foster peace. This is when you must seek God in His Word and ask the right questions: Do I have legal right within the Scriptures to separate from my spouse? Have I given all I can to fulfill my role as husband/wife? Most people will argue that divorce is not godly, and I will agree. However, staying in an abusive situation is not, either. We must be led by the Spirit and trust that God will make a way of escape for the believer. The Apostle Paul addresses this in his first letter to Corinthians 7:14-16, where he identifies the differences between the desire of the unbelieving spouse. He says, if the unbelieving spouse wants to stay, then we ought not divorce because the sanctified spouse will cover them and the children, but if they want to leave, let them leave and the sanctified spouse is not bound in this circumstance. So, if your marriage does not reflect the Passion of Christ, but all parties involved want the marriage, then allow the Holy Spirit to sanctify the union in peace. But if one does not, and has rejected the idea of oneness in the sight of God, let them go and be in peace. I believe the grace of God will honor your decision.

Is the ministry of deliverance beneficial for marriages that are in trouble?

Deliverance is beneficial in all facets of life to include marriage, especially those that are in trouble. It is likely that the enemy has placed his grips upon the union and is the culprit behind the marital disenfranchisement. Deliverance is a love ministry, and its goals are to usher in more light against darkness. The light of course is the love and Word of God, who is Jesus Christ, and the darkness is the evil one and his army.

Deliverance allows healing to flow into an area stricken by darkness and exposes all of its adversaries by the marvelous light of Truth. It is a ministry that has only honed in on the mandate given to all believers in the Great Commission to spread the Gospel, heal the sick, and cast out demons.

If we are honest with ourselves, we will acknowledge the darkness that dwells in the deepest corners of our temple [body]. This does not indicate our lack of sanctification or salvation but proves that we in fact need the Gospel every single day of our lives. Deliverance is a tool that reveals the areas that have been neglected by our worship, study, and praise. When we can deal with those areas and apply deliverance in our lives, we will make room to inhabit more of Jesus. Any time we increase the flow of Christ in our life, it will benefit everything and everyone involved. But we must be willing to acknowledge that we need to be set free, and in so doing, we will activate the liberty guaranteed by the Son of God.

"To whom the Son sets free is free indeed." John 8:36

Can a broken marriage hinder one's purpose and anointing?

The Bible says in Isaiah 54:17, "No weapon formed against you shall prosper, and every tongue that shall rise up against you in judgment shall be condemned." Therefore, every attempt by the enemy has no victory if you stand on the promises in the Word of God. But often times, believers do not operate in their spirit and fall short to the lies tormenting their flesh. So, we CAN allow ANYTHING to destroy us IF we do not trust in the Lord. The enemy's motto is to "kill, steal, and destroy..." and if we let him, that is exactly what he will do. With that said, can the enemy use a broken marriage to "kill, steal, and destroy" someone's purpose and anointing? Absolutely, but only if they allow it. The Apostle Paul understood that we as humans must die to the flesh daily in order that we maintain our truest selves in Christ Jesus. Salvation is a process that once confessed in the heart and with the tongue, the spirit is renewed but the mind and body have to catch up. And with a deceitful heart and mind full of emotions, humanity has a lot to juggle when it comes to resisting and defeating the ruler of this world. Again, the Apostle Paul took this into account and reminded us that "God has called us to live in peace" (1 Cor 7:15). If your marriage is causing you not to live in peace, you must reevaluate the circumstances and go to the altar in prayer. Sometimes, peace is in distance, other times it is in self-reflection, but it is always in repentance and humility.

For me, I sought peace in self-reflection and realized that I was not living according to my role as a wife. I decided to give my marriage and husband over to God and focus on being all that God called me to be. I fasted and prayed and developed a newness in my relationship with Christ. I learned the voice of the Holy Spirit and I started to listen to His direction. I exhausted everything I could as a righteous wife and left the rest up to God. My husband at the time rejected me and made the decision to let me go in his heart. When I asked him if he loved me, he could not answer. When he came home after months of silence and literally no contact, he had nothing left for me. I felt it and for the first time I received it.

Prior to this, I held on to previous notions of love and affection and convinced myself that deep down he still loved me and wanted our marriage. But what I never considered was that he did not. But on

February 5, 2016, I accepted the fact that he had let me go. And in an outpouring of prayer in my heavenly language, the Holy Spirit spoke on my behalf and I received peace. A month later the divorce I had hesitated with in my heart was unequivocally certain. The Holy Spirit reminded me of that moment in church a few months prior when I heard the Holy Spirit say, "That will be your last time together." It was all so clear, and I had nothing but love and peace in my heart.

Chapter 6 Questions to ponder:

Can you receive blessings while committing sin?

What God has for you is for you, and I consider that to be the premise behind what we evangelicals refer to as "favor." But mercy is a gift that is out of our hands. I believe God so graciously renders us grace and mercy when we do not deserve it, but it is not a limitless gesture.

Hebrews 9:15-16 says, "For he says to Moses, 'I will have mercy on whom I have mercy, and I will have compassion on whom I have compassion'; it does not, therefore, depend on human desire or effort, but on God's mercy."

In other words, God may bless you in the midst of your sin; however, in the case of David and Bathsheba, they lost their first son due to sin. And although what David did to acquire Bathsheba as his wife was deplorable and outside of the will and Word of God, through his repentance, God still placed "favor" upon him and blessed their union.

Obedience is always better than sacrifice. Live in God's word by speaking His language of obedience to find yourself pleasing in His sight.

I succumbed to my fleshly desires, and my current husband and I were pregnant before marriage. It was a shameful yet wonderful experience, and I grieved and thanked God. My husband had already declared that I was his wife, but I was still healing from errors from my previous relationship. But in this moment, repentance revealed my desire to be pleasing to God was greater than my desire for my need to be assured of my healing. And I decided, in prayer, to trust righteousness. I loved my baby-daddy and I did believe that he was a man of valor and God. So just like that, we made the decision to live holy and we married. It was the best decision I've ever made.

I praise God for keeping me in His grace and mercy because I clearly did not always walk in the language of obedience. But He saw fit to cover me in mercy and show me "favor," and I am eternally grateful to the Father.

Should healing occur before a new relationship or because of a new relationship?

Healing is a major topic especially when it comes to relationships. Ideally, I would argue that healing should come prior to entering into a new relationship to allow time for you to process what you have learned. But that does not always happen. Sometime we are convinced that we are healed and find out otherwise once we enter into a new relationship. And other times, God will lead us to someone who was put in position to foster healing in our lives.

Personally, all the above happened to me. I was not looking for a new relationship. It just so happened to find me during the pivotal time of my healing. I decided that all I needed was the love of God and I would give up on this "Boaz" nonsense. But God strategically placed my current husband in my path to show me that He is still the faithful God of promise. I honestly self-sabotaged the beginning of my relationship because I was convinced that I needed more time to "heal." It was my husband who reminded me that every good and perfect gift comes from the Lord, and that if God said it, it was a sure thing. My healing grew in my relationship with my husband, and I can say his did as well. But the key was to maintain an open line of communication with the Master— Christ Jesus—and actually listen to the instructions He gave.

Is peace an indicator of God's will? And can it be imitated by the enemy?

God is the epitome of peace. He is Jehovah Shalom (Judges 6:24). The author of peace and is peace Himself (2 Thessalonians 3:16; 1 Corinthians 14:33). One thing is for sure, God's peace is perfect and it cannot be replicated. However, the enemy is a counterfeit and will attempt to imitate everything of God. The Bible says he masquerades as an "angel of light," but he cannot pull off the glory of the Lord. If we are vetted in the Scriptures, then we will recognize the counterfeit attempts of the enemy.

Satan is incapable of love and therefore is incapable of peace. He will lie and deceive, but in the end, his arrogance will always boast of who he is and what he wants. Satan's goal is to destroy regardless of his façade, and that coldness will still be portrayed.

Try the spirit by the Spirit to see if it is of the Lord. If you question it, it is not God. God's peace is perfect and needs not be explained.

"We give thanks to God always for you all, making mention of you in our prayers;

Remembering without ceasing your work of faith, and labour of love, and patience of hope in our Lord Jesus Christ, in the sight of God and our Father"

1 Thessalonians 1:2-3

THANKS TO YOU …

I thank God first and foremost for giving me the strength and courage to accept the life and purpose I was given. It is only by and through God that I am able to give my testimony. God saw fit to use me as a vessel to share my love story with the world and encourage all to press towards the mark of the high calling in Christ Jesus. It is a blessing to be used by God, and I give all honor and glory to the Most High God.

A special thanks to my husband who is truly my "Promise." After searching and waiting for "Boaz" to fulfill my God-given promise to no avail; being found by Ramon was nothing more than divine. He fulfills every portion of what God promised me and I am forever grateful. You are more than supportive; you're prophetically understanding of what God placed in me. I love you so much. I also want to thank our children, Tenysia, John, Rasean, Raeah, and Rían for being the absolute joy in my heart. We have been through many storms, but we overcame them all.

I would also like to thank my family. Without you I would not have found the courage to put my life experiences into words. My mother is my rock and has always been available when and wherever I needed her. My sisters' support has been priceless and without it, I would not have made it. A special thanks to my cousin, Eletta Johnson-Williams, who believed in me from the very beginning. Because of you I took this leap of faith.

I could not end this without expressing a special thanks to my BFF. Crystal, I love you to the moon and back! I appreciate the many nights of laughing until we cried and crying until we laughed. Every road trip we took and spiritual guidance counseling session we had has been of pure joy. You are my first editor, listener, and very best friend.

To my editor J.J. Murray, I thank God for you. I appreciate all your expertise, guidance, and support. You are my brother in Christ and friend.

"Let us hold fast the profession of our hope without wavering, for He is faithful that promised." Hebrews 10:23 (KJV)

ABOUT THE AUTHOR

Marquia S. Green is dedicated to serving in the Kingdom. Called to ministry at age 15, licensed at 28, she would devote her time to study and ministry as founder of Ladies Tea Time Women's Faith Group (LTT). She earned her Bachelor of Science degree in Religion from the University of Mount Olive and is currently pursuing her Master of Theological Studies at Liberty University. Through LTT, Marquia has reached hundreds of women, educating, elevating, and strengthening them in the Word of God. Marquia is also an active member of the United States Air Force where she has served God and her country for seventeen years. She is a proud wife of a United States soldier, Ramon Green, and blended mother of five.

Made in the
USA
Columbia, SC